A River in
Egypt
Out of Denial and Into Recovery

by

G J Lewis

With special thanks;
to my parents, to Elise, and
to all at WCADA in Swansea:
The Welsh Centre for
Action on Dependency and Addiction.

Contents:

INTRODUCTION

The fact that you are reading this book suggests that you are concerned either about your own, or someone else's drinking habits or that you would simply like to learn more about problematic drinking and addiction. Either way you've probably come to the right place.

To the drinker who is concerned about their own lives, the effect they have on others when they drink and the harm they are doing to themselves, then well done. This book is by no means a one stop shop, or a cure all, but it's as good a place as any to start. You're on the right path to addressing the problems associated with your drinking and by the end of the book I hope you will have a sound understanding of how alcohol problems and or addiction affect a person and, if applicable, be able to recognise it in yourself and see through the denial that keeps so many people in an endless and ultimately terminal cycle of self destruction.

I am not a doctor or a medical professional. I am someone who has been alcohol dependant and who has recovered. I am also someone who worked for five years as a project worker in homeless hostels for individuals suffering from substance misuse issues. I have witnessed the recovery of clients who were the most hardened of alcoholics and I have seen many good people fail, many of whom are no longer with us today. Let me just say that dying from alcohol dependence or any other substance addiction is certainly not a good way to go. That said, I hope anyone currently experiencing severe anxiety after a bout of drinking, for whatever reason, finds some comfort in these pages. You are not alone and the fear will pass.

This book does feature case studies and true stories, but I will not name service providers, hostels, locations, or use any client's or colleague's real name in order to protect the identity and privacy of the people and organisations I have worked with over the years.

1.
Do I Have a Problem?

"I didn't get into trouble every time I drank, but every time I got into trouble I was drinking."[1]

Most people have had some kind of negative experience with alcohol at some point in their lives. It is when those negative experiences keep occurring that we might ask ourselves, 'do I have a problem?' According to Albert Einstein, insanity is doing the same thing over and over again and expecting a different result. If your drinking is causing you problems and you keep drinking, guess what?

The definition of problem drinking is very straight forward. It is, "any kind of drinking that causes you a problem." That's it. You

---

[1]
An anonymous person at an AA meeting

don't have to be drinking every spare minute of every day and you don't need to be spending most afternoons staggering around town roaring at pigeons. In fact you don't even need to do that sort of thing to be considered alcohol dependant.[2]

The Greater Glasgow and Clyde NHS Website,[3] provides the following basic criteria for Physical Dependency:

1. A woman who drinks 70 units or more on a regular basis.
2. A man who drinks 100 units or more on a regular basis.

At first glance it sounds like an awful lot of units but 70 units a week can be reached by sinking one bottle of wine a day. There will be times, maybe around Christmas or when on holiday abroad, that people's alcohol intake might increase to over 100 units a week, but

---

[2]

Using the term alcohol dependant is a politically correct way of saying the A word. (Alcoholic)

[3]http://www.nhsggc.org.uk/your-health/health-services/alcohol-brief-intervention/drinking-categories/dependent-drinking

when they return to their normal life their alcohol intake drops back down to 20 units a week or so. Someone who is physically dependent will drink 100 units and over on a regular basis regardless of whether they are on holiday or not. This 100 units is not necessarily consumed every week, but certainly on a regular basis. Bear in mind that the UK government guidelines for alcohol recommend a maximum of only 14 units per week for both men and women. That's just a bottle and a half of wine.

Those people who are alcohol dependant will inevitably get worse over the years, if they do not take action. It is not uncommon for people to be drinking between 200 and 300 units a week once the booze has really taken a hold. If you think you might be on that bus, it's best to get off early.

You may well be drinking far less than 100 units a week and still have a problem. I used to think I didn't have a problem, or I'd admit to having a problem then after a couple of weeks sober, convince myself that I was OK and it would start all over again.

The following statement is possibly the most important statement I have ever heard and it might be the same for you:

If you can't predict with any certainty when your drinking will end, you have a drink problem.

The above statement is much more useful than saying if you can't stick to a few drinks you have a problem because what most people tend to do is rush out, sink four pints and no more and declare that they're fine. They might be able to do that two or three more times, maybe more, but suddenly *BANG!* They wake up on the sofa surrounded by empty cans and bottles wondering what the hell happened. This is someone with a problem. They only intended to have a few but ended up absolutely smashed. If this happens on a work night, they might have slept through their alarm. They might be late for work and turn up bleary eyed and stinking of booze, or they might just throw a sickie. If not working or not working that day, they might just keep going. Having a quiet drink has turned into an entirely unpredictable continuous bender and it all started with the first sip. If that sort of thing happens to you, the only sure way to prevent it from happening is not to drink anything at all.

Is drink really worth it? Is it worth losing your job over? Is it worth splitting up with your partner over? Is it worth ending up homeless, in prison, hospital or a mental facility? Those examples might sound extreme but that is the sort of thing that can and often does happen to people who do not take control of their drinking.

I have listed below some true examples of the negative impact of alcohol on my life;

    1. Suffering more blackouts than a Londoner in the Blitz.

    2. Constantly hopping jobs due to sickness levels.

    3. Being arrested for drunk & disorderly.

    4. Getting into fights with strangers.

    5. Numerous relationship breakdowns.

    6. Drink driving.

7. Disgracing myself at work socials, in pubs and just about everywhere else.

8. Having the police called on me by terrified people in a pub. (Threatening behaviour.)

9. Being badly beaten and hospitalised.

10. Receiving an abnormal liver test result.

11. Drinking day and night for days and sometimes weeks at a time.

12. Losing my job.

13. Not going out of the house. (Only to the shop to buy drink)

14. Suffering paranoia, severe anxiety, heart palpitations and hearing things.

15. Regularly suffering from shakes and other withdrawal symptoms.

16. Severe depression and suicidal ideology.

I could go on but I think you get the picture. The really shocking thing is that after all that, I still thought I wasn't that bad, that I wasn't an alcoholic and that I could keep drinking. It wasn't until I was threatened with a mental health section and evicted from my home that I really put my foot down and said, 'that's it, I don't need this shit in my life any more.'

You might not be that bad, yet. I started off drinking at the weekends with my friends like most people do. It was fun, social and for a good few years the entire weekend was one big booze-fuelled adventure. Who'd want to give that up? I lived for that release at the end of the week.

The thing is no one wants to have a problem with alcohol. No one wants to become mentally and physically dependant, but over time a certain proportion of people become just that. The weekend starts to stretch out. Thursday is nearly the weekend so weekend starts here. One bottle of wine on a work night is fine... actually, make it two. After all red wine's meant to be good for you, right? Slowly, as the condition develops, the good times become less and less and the excuses mount. The vast majority of problem drinkers end up drinking alone in an ever increasing cycle of isolation and self destruction.

Why do we let this happen to ourselves? The trouble with most drinkers is that they are in denial of the true extent of their drink problem. I certainly was. Many people use alcohol as a go to solution for all of life's problems and many people suffering from an underlying mental health condition use it to self medicate, to drown out the stress, the anger, the depression, anxiety and general frustration that they encounter in their day to day lives. Going sober and staying sober is about learning to cope with everything life can throw at you without turning to drink. It's difficult, but it's very achievable. Just think of yourself being able to cope with everything, absolutely everything life can throw at you, without picking up a drink. That's one confident, resilient human being.

If we can truly face the fact that we can't drink like most other people, that we have a problem and that we need help, there is no need to go all the way to the bottom. You can get off the ride at any time. Then again, one won't hurt, will it?

Just remember that when someone gets hit by a set of runaway train carriages, it's not the seventh or eighth carriage that kills them, it's always the first. The rest of the carriages rolling over them just make a right bloody mess!

2.
Denial

There were two men at a funeral…
'How did he die?'
'It was the booze.'
'So he was an alcoholic?'
'Nah, he wasn't that bad.'

Welcome to Egypt!

The Nile or De-Nile is also a river in Egypt. Apart from vaguely rhyming with denial, the Nile's only similarity with drink problems is that the river mouth sees approximately 3.1 million litres (680,000 gallons) of liquid pass through it every second.[4]

---

[4]http://africa-facts.org/nile-river-facts/

Now back to the serious stuff…

Denial is the number one reason why people do not address the reality of their relationship with alcohol. Denial comes both from the drinker and from those around the drinker, but it is only the person who has a problem that needs to overcome denial. Only then can they admit the true extent of their problem to themselves and to others.

Do not worry about what anyone else thinks, it is only the self that can be truly honest with its-self. Not caring about what anyone else thinks will also serve someone well if they are already in recovery. Keep the focus on your own thoughts, feelings and actions. Most of the time, everyone else is too busy worrying about themselves and their own problems anyway.

If we are to get to the heart of denial, a good place to start is the Oxford English Dictionary which defines it as follows: *"refusal to acknowledge an unacceptable truth or emotion."*[5] So the question we need to ask is: 'why is it unacceptable to the drinker to admit to themselves and to others that they have a drink problem?'

---

[5]PKT OED. 9th Ed (Oxford University Press 2002)

There is no easy answer to this due to the complexity of each individual human psyche, however we all have similarities so I shall have a go at answering it:

Many people use alcohol to alleviate stress, past trauma, anxiety and depression. In this sense we can say that many people use alcohol as self medication, a way of coping with the world and their feelings.

Despite the fact that drinking too much alcohol actually makes stress, anxiety and depression much worse and often leads to additional trauma, alcohol fools our minds into thinking that a good binge will help. This then manifests as a strong craving for a drink which if not satisfied makes the user feel desperate and even more stressed, anxious and depressed. When the user finally gets a drink the feeling of relief is massive.

In addition to the psychological relief, the brain releases a flood of endorphins, the body's natural reward mechanism, which temporarily lifts the drinker's mood and joins the depressant properties of the alcohol in relaxing the body, reinforcing both physically and mentally the falsehood that alcohol is the drinkers friend. Even if later on in the same drinking session the drinker has a very negative experience, the brain has both consciously and subconsciously remembered the 'reward' of earlier. This then perpetuates the self destructive cycle that blinds the drinker to the harm being done to themselves and those around them.

There is also a societal element to denial which is multifaceted yet easy to understand. Basically, no one wants to be seen as the town drunk. We are programmed by society to the extent that the word 'alcoholic' conjures up images of heavily bearded tramps shouting at squirrels in the park, when the fact of the matter is that most alcoholics blend right into a society in which drinking alcohol is a normal social activity. Our denial of our true relationship with alcohol can therefore also be seen as a defence mechanism against the perceived prejudice within society. Ironically the problem drinker / alcoholic who is so worried about what society thinks is also more than likely quite fed up with society to say the least. Please see the quote below in which I draw your attention to the last two words in particular:

"What is it about society that disappoints you so much?

...Oh I don't know, is it that we collectively thought Steve Jobs was a great man even when we knew he made billions off the backs of children?

Or maybe it's that it feels like all our heroes are counterfeit; the world itself's just one big hoax. Spamming each other with our burning commentary of bullshit masquerading as insight, our social media faking as intimacy.

Or is it that we voted for this? Not with our rigged elections, but with our things, our property, our money. I'm not saying anything new. We all know why we do this, not because Hunger Games books makes us happy but because we wanna be sedated. Because it's painful not to pretend, because we're cowards.

Fuck Society."[6]

So that's the central character Elliot responding to a question posed by his shrink in Sam Ismael's Mr Robot. I haven't only

---

[6] Mr Robot [TV Series] Season 1, Episode 1 (2015)

included it because I like it, I've included it because I believe the problem drinker can take something from it. Denial is not only something that's happening to addicts, it is a phenomenon that is happening to the whole of society in multiple guises and, lets face it, the world needs to wake up.

Step away from what society thinks about you. Society has enough of it's own problems and the individuals within it are all concentrating on their little piece of the puzzle within their own bubbles. Concentrate on your piece of the puzzle and regardless of your past make a better future for yourself and those around you. This can only start once you are honest with yourself. It starts with the truth, your truth, and it takes courage.

Other 'Bars' to Recovery...

Denial is just one of many obstacles to overcome on the path to recovery. Often people know they have a serious problem but continue to drink anyway. This is either for psychological reasons, physical reasons, or a mixture of the two.

Conversely, the physical reason for continuing to drink can be a valid one. Sudden withdrawal from alcohol can prove fatal where there is a serious physical addiction or where the individual has been drinking continuously for a number of days or more. Always seek medical advice before trying to stop.

www.drugs.com provides the following guide to symptoms associated with withdrawal:

"If your brain has adjusted to your heavy drinking habits, it takes time for your brain to adjust back. Alcohol withdrawal symptoms occur in a predictable pattern after your last alcohol drink. Not all symptoms develop in all patients:

- **Tremors (shakes)** — These usually begin within 5 to 10 hours after the last alcohol drink and typically peak at 24 to 48 hours. Along with tremors (trembling), you can have a rapid pulse, an increase in blood pressure, rapid breathing, sweating, nausea and vomiting, anxiety or a hyper-alert state, irritability, nightmares or vivid dreams, and insomnia.

- **Alcohol hallucinosis** — This symptom usually begins within 12 to 24 hours after your last drink, and may last as long as 2 days once it begins. If this happens, you hallucinate (see or feel things that are not real). It is common for people who are withdrawing from alcohol to see multiple small, similar, moving objects. Sometimes the vision is perceived to be crawling insects or falling coins. It is possible for an alcohol withdrawal hallucination to be a very detailed and imaginative vision.

- **Alcohol withdrawal seizures** — Seizures may occur 6 to 48 hours after the last drink, and it is common for several seizures to occur over several hours. The risk peaks at 24 hours.

- **Delirium tremens** — Delirium tremens commonly begins two to three days after the last alcohol drink, but it may be delayed more than a week. Its peak intensity is usually four to five days after the last drink. This condition causes dangerous shifts in your breathing, your circulation and your temperature control. It can cause your heart to race dangerously or can cause your blood pressure to increase dramatically, and it can cause dangerous dehydration. Delirium tremens can also temporarily reduce the amount of blood flow to your brain. Symptoms can include confusion, disorientation, stupor or loss of consciousness, nervous or angry behaviour, irrational beliefs, soaking sweats, sleep disturbances and hallucinations."[7]

---

[7]https://www.drugs.com/health-guide/alcohol-withdrawal.html

If your withdrawal is as severe as Delirium Tremens (DT's) or you have experienced a seizure (even if it was a long time ago), you need to get to a medical facility as soon as possible. Once there, it is likely that benzodiazepines will be given to alleviate your symptoms if those symptoms are deemed to be severe enough. If you are dead against drugs and do not want to take a drug to get better, remember that alcohol is also a drug and just because it's legal, doesn't make you any less of a drug addict. Alcohol is also one of the only drugs that can kill you if you go cold turkey. The mortality rate among patients exhibiting alcohol withdrawal symptoms in the form of DT's is 5 to 25 percent.[8] Benzodiazepine's are usually only prescribed on a rapid taper due to their addictive nature and they are the most widely used and effective treatment for severe alcohol withdrawal symptoms.

*

---

[8]Louis A. Trevisan, M.D., Nashaat Boutros, M.D., Ismene L. Petrakis, M.D., and John H. Krystal, M.D. Complications of Alcohol Withdrawal: Pathophysiological Insights, (1998) p62 Vol. 22, No.1

Psychological reasons for continuing to drink are more difficult to fix than the physical. This is often due to a loss of hope in the drinker who is more than likely suffering from some form of depression. This depression may be an underlying cause of, or a result of, the effects of prolonged heavy drinking. Either way it's very real.

> "Depressive symptoms often are observed in patients who are intoxicated or undergoing alcohol detoxification. As many as 15 percent of alcoholics are at risk of death by suicide..."[9]

To put this into context, the World Health Organisation (2015) estimates that the suicide rate amongst the general global population is approximately 0.016%. Looking at the cold numbers we can see that someone suffering from alcoholism is up to 1000 times more likely to commit suicide than the average person. The link between alcoholism and depression couldn't be clearer but whether it was the chicken or the egg that came first depends very much on the individual.

---

[9]As above. p63

We can see both from the physical and psychological pit falls of both drinking and coming off drink, that medical advice is a must. As well as the potential for physical withdrawal issues, your mental health also needs to be looked after and could be considered even more important. After all it's your mind that will keep you sober or keep you drunk. There is no shame in asking for help and a good place to start is always your local doctor. Please also see the support index at the back of this book for the contact details of support agencies listed by country.

3.

Jekyll & Hyde

"Between these two, I now felt I had to choose."[10]

*

Most people have heard of, seen or read Robert Louis Stevenson's classic tale of a man losing himself to his evil alter ego after drinking a 'potion'. Those of us who have ever acted like a mad man or woman after too much to drink, or witnessed the same in someone else, will easily be able to see the the inspiration behind Stevenson's novel.

---

[10]Stevenson, Robert Louis. *The Strange Case of Dr. Jekyll and Mr. Hyde*. New York: Scribner, 1886; Chapter 10, Paragraph 16.

There is of course a big difference between this fictional story of a doctor using an invented compound to free his repressed darker nature, and the reality of alcoholism. In the original book, Dr Jekyll could always remember what he had done whilst under the influence of the potion and he actually wanted the freedom of this uninhibited behaviour. What many drinkers find when their behaviour has been extreme is that they can't remember anything, or if they can remember, that their memory is hazy or fragmented. When they are told about how they behaved the night before they are often horrified, their actions being unintended. Drinkers also don't have the luxury of a different body to 'hide' in during a big binge. See why the doctors alter ego was called Hyde?

If when you drink you are prone to blackouts and uncharacteristic or even violent behaviour, then the only thing to do is not drink in the first place. If you are prone to this kind of behaviour it is not acceptable to continually blame the alcohol because it was you who consciously made the decision to drink in the knowledge that you risked behaving badly.

So just like the good Dr Jekyll had to do, you have to choose. Do you want to be Dr Jekyll or Mr Hyde? The more times people see you as Mr or Ms Hyde and the more times you allow yourself to become that darker personality, the more you become it. Put the genie back in the bottle or keep on going and become Hyde. The choice is yours.

Blackouts...

Most heavy drinkers will have experienced an alcohol induced blackout at some point in their lives and might be familiar with the feelings of dread and fear that result from one. Not knowing what you said or did is a horrible feeling, especially if you don't have anyone who can tell you what happened. The natural human thing to do is to think the worse and many people spend days or weeks after a blackout in a state of high anxiety often when nothing untoward occurred – Then again maybe it did?

The part of the brain that deals with the storing of real lifetime events is heavily affected by alcohol and if enough is consumed this memory process switches off altogether until the blood alcohol level drops back to a manageable level. Flickering can also occur where the memory function of the brain switches on and off fairly rapidly meaning that people forget what they've just said two minutes ago and repeat and repeat the same drunken crap all night long. This also creates a fragmented memory of the night before. People say things like, I remember getting to the bar, then I was playing pool but it was dark outside already, then nothing until I woke up. Now, whether or not something bad happened, for your brain something bad did happen. It has events, 1,2,3,.....7,...9.... then nothing until you wake up. So what does it do? It takes the best guess to fill in the gaps so you get events 1,2,3,(4)(5)(6)7 etc even though 4, 5 and 6 didn't even happen. This is known as confabulation and is exactly the same as what happens in the brain of someone suffering from Korzecauffs syndrome or alcoholic dementia. Scary isn't it? Unless your memory of the night before comes back to you quickly, you can't trust what you might start to remember later on, especially if all you're doing is hiding away from the world whilst your mind runs riot. This works both ways, possibly making you think you did nothing wrong when you did and making you

think you did something terrible when you
didn't.

If anyone is actually reading this directly after
suffering a blackout, know that if you did do
something that bad you'd have woken up in a
prison cell or to a knock at the door, so try
and stay calm and know that you will feel
normal again. If you are already trying or
thinking about quitting, write down the terror
that you're experiencing and next time you
feel like a drink, read it.

4.

The Nature of Addiction

"Religion is the opiate of the masses." Karl
Marx

"I did masses of opiates religiously." Carrie
Fisher

1. Addiction as a Disease

Whether or not you believe alcoholism and
other serious substance misuse issues to be
actual illnesses, many addictions share strong
similarities with chronic disease. For
example, diabetes and alcoholism share the
following:

1. They are progressive, they get worse over
time.

2. They require a change in behaviour.

3. Patients can relapse, with the return of symptoms that are often worse than before.

4. There is a genetic element.

5. There is no cure.

6. If left unchecked they are terminal.

Lets look at some case studies and then you can decide for yourself. There's no right answer.

CASE STUDY 1

Client X had been drinking for his entire adult life. His drinking started on an occasional weekend basis when he was a teenager and progressed through his twenties and early thirties. It was a social thing and he wasn't doing anything different to his peers. As he got older the drinking spread from the weekends into the week days. Before he stopped drinking he was consuming approximately 50 units of alcohol a day in the week and even more at the weekends. He had a good job but it was a job that saw him out in the fresh air more often than not, so others couldn't smell the alcohol on his breath as much as they would if he had been office based. This allowed his consumption of alcohol to continue for an extended period of time before crisis point was reached.

Client X was admitted to hospital after being found unconscious and with the skin colour of Bart Simpson. For a time it looked like he wasn't going to make it but thankfully he pulled through. His liver was severely scarred and the vast majority of it was no longer functional. He was able to survive on the remaining part that would regenerate to some extent as long as he never drank again. Client X drank again.

CASE STUDY 2

Client X was a young man with a good but stressful job. He was also a binge drinker. After a stressful day he'd drink 1-2 bottles of red wine and after a stressful week he'd spend the entire weekend drinking lager in the local pub. At the age of twenty Client X decided to prove to himself that he was not an alcoholic by giving up alcohol for 1 month. He managed this with no real problems and then celebrated the fact that he wasn't an alcoholic with a great big booze up with his friends.

10 years later Client X was still binge drinking heavily. He would often throw up yellow bile in the mornings and suffered from severe anxiety and shakes after a drinking session. After feeling very unwell for a period of time client X went to the doctor who took bloods. This resulted in an abnormal liver result being returned. Client X was advised that he should cut down on alcohol and that if he couldn't cut down he should quit altogether or risk death within 2 years. Knowing he had a real problem, client X decided to quit drinking altogether. It lasted 3 months. Client X soon found he was drinking even more than

before. He quit again and this period lasted 8 months. After this client X found himself drinking yet even more. Eventually he was fired from his job, evicted from his home and threatened with a mental health section before he finally understood the nature of his problem. Client X was an alcoholic. He sought help from his local GP and took all referrals given to him. He was told he had a disease and that it wasn't his fault, all he had to do was not drink and use the help offered. Client X later learned that there were at least two known alcoholics on his fathers side of the family. Client X is still sober.

CASE STUDY 3

Client X entered into a dry hostel environment in order to try and stop himself from drinking. He was sober for a period of 12 months and showed himself to be a friendly, well liked and good natured individual who was progressing well in his sober life. Having a background in computer science, Client X managed to land himself a job in the IT department of a major television broadcaster. Everything was looking up and he seemed to be thriving in his new role.

Without warning client X failed to return to the hostel or to work. We quickly learned that he had relapsed and was staying with a friend where he was able to drink. Client X appeared outside the hostel one night, drunk, aggressive and violent. The friendly, intelligent, good natured man we all knew was gone, our Dr Jekyll had become his alter ego. Within 3 months client X was dead.

*

The above case studies are all completely true and are not meant to tell you anything but the truth. Unfortunately I have many more of them that are not included here.

In relation to how best to treat substance misuse issues, there is mounting evidence and ongoing research projects that suggest that treating alcoholism and other addictions as a disease improves outcomes for patients and this has been known for at least 20 years. So in other words, if your doctor tells you that you have a terminal, incurable, disease, and that you need treatment for it, you are more likely to stay sober than if he tells you that you're simply addicted to alcohol and that you need to mend your ways.

"Extensive research has shown that treatment for addiction is as effective as treatments for other chronic, relapsing medical conditions." [11]

One reason why this is so is a matter of psychology. If you tell someone they have a disease, then the blame is lifted from their shoulders. However, if that person acknowledges they have a disease and continues to drink or returns to drink after a period of sobriety, then the blame is firmly back on their shoulders. This then makes it more likely that the individual who has stopped drinking and fully accepted that they have the 'illness', will remain sober as they do not want the burden of blame to return after it had been, to some extent, alleviated.

So good news bad news. It's best to think of your addiction as an incurable chronic

---

[11]Institute of Medicine. Dispelling the Myths About Addiction: Strategies to Increase Understanding and Strengthen Research (1997) p87

disease, but you can get better and you can stay better.

2. An Alternative Theory: Rat Park

In the late 1970's, psychologist professor Bruce K. Alexander & his colleagues at Simon Fraser University in Canada, conducted a series of experiments that produced a theory of addiction that came to be named 'Rat Park.'

During the experiment, rats in solitary confinement were compared to rats living in a large enclosure known as Rat Park. The large enclosure was a purpose built environment full of things rats like, such as platforms for climbing, tin cans for hiding in, wood chips for strewing around, and running wheels for exercise. In Rat Park there were also lots of rats of both sexes, and naturally the place soon was teeming with babies.

In both the solitary cages and Rat Park, the rats had food, a water bottle and a bottle containing morphine solution. The rats in solitary took to the morphine straight away, and quickly developed a strong habit, in some cases drinking themselves to death. In Rat Park however, although the rats used the morphine bottle they used it a lot less, a hell of a lot less, in fact you could say they used it recreationally.

There is obviously a great leap from rats to humans but one event in history can be used to draw comparisons between studies. During the Vietnam War many US soldiers enduring the daily horrors of combat, took to using opiates such as morphine which came in their medi kits and subsequently heroine and opium that they sourced locally. When it came to returning home after the war a good number of men were addicted to opiates, but for most the addiction did not continue once on home soil. They had been removed from the oppressive environment that had led them to use in the first place and felt able to live their lives without their crutch. 95% of soldiers addicted to narcotics in Vietnam broke the habit when they returned home:

"1/5 of the enlisted troops were addicted at some time during their tour. The major contributing factors appear to be: (1) the need of troops in stressful combat situations for self-medication, escape, and hedonistic indulgence; (2) the relaxation of taboos against drug use in the United States; and (3) the availability of illicit drugs at low cost, which was apparently the result of profiteering by a number of South Vietnamese officials. Related to the above was the growing disenchantment with the war and the progressive deterioration in unit morale. These drugs are seen as serving many of the functions performed by alcohol in earlier millitary conflicts. There is no hard evidence that duty performance in Vietnam was seriously affected by drug use. Since 95% of those who were addicted to narcotics in Vietnam have not become readdicted..."[12]

[12]US National Library of Medicine: Am J Drug Alcohol Abuse. (1976) 3 (4) p557-70

Image from Rat Park, with thanks to Professor Bruce Alexander.[13]

---

[13]http://www.brucekalexander.com/articles-speeches/rat-park/148-addiction-the-view-from-rat-park

3. The Nature of Addiction: Conclusion

From the evidence we have looked at we can see that there is no easy answer to whether addiction is a disease or something born of environment and circumstance. Like many things in life it does not have to be one or the other, it is in fact a mix of the two. In this sense we can say that both theories on addiction are correct, that some people are pre-disposed to addictive behaviour and can be said to have a 'disease', but also that their circumstances and environment come into play in forming that behaviour.

Some might assume that there are different types of addict, those of circumstance and those who have the disease, but again, it's not that simple. We can see from the Vietnam study on the previous page that 95% of soldiers addicted to opiates whilst in Vietnam ceased to be addicts once they had returned home. 5% did not manage to kick the habit. That alone is not evidence enough to assume that the 5% who continued to take opiates had the disease of addiction and that the other 95% did not. This is due to the fact that we do not know what kind of environment the soldiers were returning to, and we do not know what psychological and or physical harm had been inflicted upon them whilst they served their country.

Here's some interesting data taken from the National Institute for Drug Abuse in the USA which shows relapse rates for drug addiction compared to other conditions.[14]

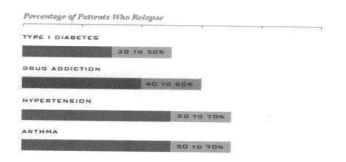

Percentage of Patients Who Relapse

TYPE I DIABETES
20 TO 50%

DRUG ADDICTION
40 TO 60%

HYPERTENSION
50 TO 70%

ASTHMA
50 TO 70%

[14]NIDA. "Principles of Drug Addiction Treatment: A Research-Based Guide (Third Edition)." *NATIONAL INSTITUTE ON DRUG ABUSE,* 17 Jan. 2018, https://www.drugabuse.gov/publications/principles-drug-addiction-treatment-research-based-guide-third-edition.

Looking more closely at the severity of drug
addiction before, during and after treatment in
comparison to hypertension over the same
period of time, we can see that the graphs are
almost identical. [15]

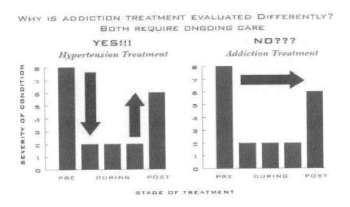

The hard data from the disease models
coupled with the data from Rat Park and the
Vietnam study clearly show that both the
disease and the environmental models are
completely correct. It remains a mystery as to
what proportion of each is in the mix, an
enigma as to exactly what extent each plays in
the formation of a drug or alcohol
dependency. About as exact as we can get is
to say it's a bit of both and that the amount

[15]Ibid

each contributes to the condition varies from person to person. This variance in contributing factors leads us to the conclusion that treatment options for substance misuse issues should be tailored to the individual. Horses for courses as the old saying goes.

5.

Methods of Recovery

In this quick guide I will outline the two methods that I have direct experience of, both as a support practitioner and as a recovering alcoholic, namely the abstinence method as central to the 12 Step, and the control method.

1. **Twelve Step Programs (Total Abstinence)**

One of the most popular methods of recovery is the 12 Step program and variations of it. You will most likely have heard of AA - Alcoholics Anonymous, which was the original 12 Step recovery program that has now been adapted to include NA – Narcotics Anonymous & CA – Cocaine Anonymous to name but two of the many off shoots from the original AA program. Many residential rehab centres also offer 12 Step Programs, be it AA, NA or sometimes a customised in house 12 Step Variation. Before I get into the pro's and con's of this method of recovery I'll get right to the heart of the matter, the original 12 Steps of AA:

The 12 Steps

1. **We admitted we were powerless over alcohol - that our lives had become unmanageable.**

2. **Came to believe that a Power greater than ourselves could restore us to sanity.**

3. **Made a decision to turn our will and our lives over to the care of God as we understood Him.**

4. **Made a searching and fearless moral inventory of ourselves.**

5. **Admitted to God, to ourselves and to another human being the exact nature of our wrongs.**

6. **Were entirely ready to have God remove all these defects of character.**

7. **Humbly asked Him to remove our shortcomings.**

8. **Made a list of all persons we had harmed, and became willing to make amends to them all.**

9. **Made direct amends to such people wherever possible, except when to do so would injure them or others.**

10. **Continued to take personal inventory and when we were wrong promptly admitted it.**

11. **Sought through prayer and meditation to improve our conscious contact with God as we understood Him, praying only for knowledge of His will for us and the power to carry that out.**

12. **Having had a spiritual awakening as the result ofthese steps, we tried to carry this message to alcoholics and to practice these principles in all our affairs.**[16]

The first thing you'll notice from reading the steps is that they form an abstinence based method of recovery and a spiritual method of recovery. The spiritual element can put some people off, but even if you're an atheist you can get something out of attending AA or NA meetings.

---

[16]https://www.alcoholics-anonymous.org.uk/about-aa/the-12-steps-of-aa

It is the first step that is the most important and it is a step that requires belief in nothing other than your own truth:

"We admitted we were powerless over alcohol - that our lives had become unmanageable."

Or if you're addicted to opiates:

"We admitted we were powerless over opiates - that our lives had become unmanageable."

Or cocaine:

"We admitted we were powerless over cocaine - that our lives had become unmanageable."

Or anything you can get your hands on:

"We admitted we were powerless over drink & drugs - that our lives had become unmanageable."

As well as being a spiritual method of recovery, 12 Step Programs are almost always done in a group setting and therefore have a social element to them. The gatherings of people on the path of recovery are called meetings and these meetings occur in just about every major city & town on the planet. At these meetings the 12 Steps are read out, often followed by a reading from 'The Big Blue Book' which has in it the stories of the founders of the AA program who were all themselves alcoholics. This is then followed by sharing, where people talk to the whole group about their addiction and how it has affected their lives. If you don't want to speak you don't have to. The most important thing at these meetings is to listen.

Listen for the similarities between yourself and the speakers and try not to focus too much on your differences. If you have an addiction problem you will hear your truth in the mouths of others, which might lead you to realise that you are 'one of them.' This then helps you to both realise and accept the extent of your own substance misuse issue and in doing so overcome one of the hurdles of denial.

Another aspect of AA is the Sponsor system. This is when an experienced member of the group takes you under their wing to work through the steps with you and generally keep you on the straight and narrow.

Personally I no longer attend AA meetings as I'm basically an anti-social hill dweller, but I did get something from the meetings I did attend in the early days of my recovery. It's always good to know you're not alone and that the door is always open.

12 Step Pro's:

*Huge network of support with AA meetings across the globe.

*Highly effective for those who take to the program

*Well established & well known.

*Excellent for people comfortable in group settings.

*Can be a good introduction to the possibilities offered by spiritual
recovery.

*Anonymity is a core value

12 Step Con's:

*It's not for everyone.

12 Step Conclusion:

Although it's not for everyone, those who take to it and seriously work the steps do very well. The many meetings I attended in my early days of recovery formed a basis for my continued recovery and I would therefore recommend that anyone who is suffering from an addiction problem, problematic substance misuse, or even a behavioural issue such as gambling, attend a good few meetings, be it AA, NA, CA, GA and so on. Give it a go, just go along to a meeting and listen.

2. Control Methods of Recovery

Control methods generally relate to substances that are capable of being used socially or recreationally. For example alcohol is used in a controlled way by most people and control methods aim to return the problem drinker to a level of drinking that is non problematic or at least less harmful.

Substances such as heroine are generally not included in control methods due to the highly addictive nature of the drug and its illegal status making non problematic use more difficult to achieve. That said, harm reduction is available and useful for any substance.

For substances such as alcohol, control methods sometimes take the form of requiring a sustained period of abstinence, from a few months to a couple of years, followed by a return to controlled drinking with certain rules in place, such as no alcohol in the home, or only drinking with company, to try and stop the return to problem drinking. Cognitive Behavioural Therapy (CBT) can be used to unlearn unhealthy habits, along with counselling and even hypnotherapy, however all of these are also available for complete abstinence systems.

The obvious problem with control methods is that full relapse or a one off catastrophic incident are a constant risk. If you have developed a serious problem with alcohol your brain's capacity to moderate is permanently damaged along with other brain functions, but this does improve over time:

"The good news is that for people in recovery from alcohol problems, many difficulties with concentration and memory will improvesubstantially in the first month of recovery, and even throughout continued recovery as long as you stay away from alcohol."[17]

Control Method Pro's

　　*Less intimidating to the problem drinker than complete
　　abstinence.

　　*A good starting point

　　*No need for total abstinence if control is possible.

Control Method Con's

　　*You might still end up drunk.

　　*Full Relapse is an obvious risk.

---

[17]https://www.psychologytoday.com/us/blog/addiction-science/200810/what-does-alcohol-do-your-brain

Conclusion:

As you might have gathered from the above pro's and cons, I'm not a big advocate of the control method. This is more than likely due to my personal bias as abstinence is what works for me and I therefore believe the control method to be a cop-out, however many respected people would disagree with me and I'll admit that it does seem to work for some people. If you are unsure what method is right for you or if you're just not ready to cut drink out your life for good the control method is definitely a good place to start and certainly worth doing. If the control method fails you still have the option of the abstinence method.

Ultimately it is only the person concerned who can decide what's right for them, so if abstinence doesn't sound like your thing right now, please try the control method, bearing in mind that the quote on the previous page about the recovery of the brain should tell you all you need to know, that you will get better "...as long as you stay away from alcohol."[18]

---

[18]Ibid

6.

Things That Help

1. Meditation

Meditation is something that has been practised for thousands of years by those seeking spiritual enlightenment or those seeking to find their true selves. Today meditation is used more widely for inner reflection, to find inner peace and as a tool of therapy for various ailments both physical and mental, as well as maintaining it's place in the tool box of the spiritually minded.

During deep meditation people often experience seeing waves or pulses of colour, the inner or third eye and unexplained visions. Some people have even encountered entities known or unknown or received some kind of message, spoken or otherwise.

I recently watched a documentary talk hosted by the legendary comedian John Cleese that posed the question 'Is there life after death?'[19] The panel consisted of Scientists & Doctors from UVA's Division of Perceptual Studies and one of those panelists had an interesting story about how meditation had helped one of her patients. The patient in question was an alcoholic who had tried everything to try and stop his chronic drinking but had been unable to stop. With all traditional avenues exhausted, the doctor prescribed him a course of mindfulness meditation and after some time something happened. During an episode of meditation the patient heard a scolding voice telling him off for drinking and telling him to pack it in. The patient believed the voice may have been that of his mother whom I assume was departed. The doctor confirmed that the patient was not delusional and that this voice the patient heard during meditation was the only thing that had managed to stop him drinking.

[19]https://www.youtube.com/watch?v=4RGizqsLumo

Meditation Method

Put your phone on silent or feed it to the waste disposal and find a quiet place where you will not be disturbed. Sit down on a chair, sofa, beanbag or the floor in an upright and comfortable position with your hands palm down on your thighs or pressed together as if in prayer. It is better to sit upright than to lie down as there is a tendency to fall asleep if you're lying down flat on your back.

Once in position close your eyes and start to breathe in through your nose and out through your mouth. Rhythmic breathing is sometimes used where you breathe in for 4 beats, then out for 4 beats and so on. This is taking conscious control of your breathing.

Keeping your eyes closed and continuing to breathe in through the nose and out through the mouth, focus your concentration or energy at the area of your forehead between your eyes.

Try and relax as much as possible, keep your eyes closed, keep breathing and try and keep your focus on the area of your forehead between your eyebrows. Let thoughts and images rise but always try and bring your focus back to your centre.

The aim is to meditate for an hour at a time but just try it for twenty minutes to start with and build it up slowly. Eventually the thoughts become less and less and a misty shimmering ring of colour might appear. This is the third eye, the sight beyond sight and the beginning of the inner journey.

2. Exercise

I won't say too much on this one as we all know that exercise is good for us but we all also know it can be a real chore. If it's not your thing the trick is to start small and build it up slowly.

The benefits of regular exercise on mental health and general well-being are well established so some kind of regular exercise is almost essential in maintaining recovery.

Jogging is an obvious choice that doesn't require anything more than a t-shirt, some jogging bottoms and a pair of trainers. All you have to do is open the door and jog away for 5 minutes then jog back. Build it up slowly until you can run away from home for half an hour like someone fleeing Amityville.

If staying in is more your thing there's squats, sit ups, crunches, press ups, pull ups, yoga, pilates, you name it. Same as everything start small and build it up.

3. Diet

When I was drinking I didn't have a sweet tooth at all, but as soon as I went sober I got right into it. Ice-cream, chocolate, milkshakes, coca cola, anything I fancied as long as it wasn't alcoholic.

The good news is that in the early stages of recovery I recommend treating yourself to whatever you fancy, just make sure you burn some of it off with a bit of exercise or you'll end up being taken to hospital by an industrial crane.

As your recovery progresses you can get a bit stricter with yourself and look into a proper healthy diet, but the most important thing is to stay away from your poison of choice so don't beat yourself up if you have the odd ice-cream too many.

Supplements are also important as many people who have a substance misuse issue are missing vital vitamins and minerals that were either not consumed or that the body used up or expelled during the period of use.

A good all round multivitamin is highly recommended and for the alcoholics an additional vitamin B complex might be required to help support normal brain function. A melatonin supplement might also be helpful to help you sleep.

Whatever vitamin or other supplement you decide to take, clear it with your doctor first, especially if you're on other medication or if you have liver, heart or kidney problems.

7.

Goodbye & Good Luck

This short book is now drawing to a close. I hope you have found something interesting in the pages it contains and that you have seen within it something that will help you in whatever situation you are in.

The road to and of recovery is a long one but it's a road you must take if you are one of those people this book is aimed at, that is if you want to lead a better life for yourself and others.

A little note to end on the spiritual side of life. It's very easy to think there's nothing out there, especially in this world where bad things happen to good people all of the time. I think the truth is that there is a God but that He (I believe God has no gender and both genders all at once but I use He to make things easier to write) is not an interventionist God in the biblical sense. He is however a source of strength, a being of light that can dispel the darkness in times of need on a psychological level.

That said we are in a chaotic Universe on a planet where anything can happen to anyone both good and bad and no one's going to hold your hand through all the shit on this side of the veil or the other. The thing is through meditation and or prayer you might start to create a little link, like a golden strand of hair to that source of light I call God, and it's in brief moments when something happens that's unexplained that you realise that you do actually matter, even in this chaotic infinite Universe on this slowly dying planet run by profiteering morally bankrupt fuck pigs.

Why am I so sure there's a God? Because I once drank so much alcohol and dropped so many pills that my heart stopped. It was a voice in the darkness that pulled me out of hell flying up back into my body, but I guess that's another story.

God bless.

Global AA Support Directory

(https://www.alcoholics-anonymous.org.uk/aa-worldwide)

EUROPE

Austria
1030 Wien. Barthgasse 5
Phone (43) 1 799 5599
Website www.anonyme-alkoholiker.at

Belarus
The Byelorussian Service Office Of A.A.
Pritytskogo Str. 60/1-331
Minsk, 220121
Belarus
Phone 375 29-276-83-17
Fax 375 17-206-7914
Website aabelarus.org

Belgium
Flemish Speaking:-
Algemeen Dienstbureau A.A.s
Grote Steenweg 149
Antwerp, 2600, Belgium
Phone 32-3-239-1415

French Speaking-
Bureau des Services Généraux
rue des pieds d'alouette 42
Naninne, 5100, Belgium

Bruxelles, 01000, Belgium
Phone 32-2-5114030
Website Flemish www.aavlaanderen.org
Website French www.alcooliquesanonymes.be

Bulgaria
Central Service Office Of A.A.
Office 14
71, Zahari Knyajeski Str
Stara Zagora City 6000, Bulgaria
Phone (359) 877 707 122
Website: www.aa-bg.info

Croatia
A.A. Central Office Zagrebu
Vrbnicka 28
Zagreb 100000
Phone (385)91-9558993
Fax (385)13-843449
Website www.aahrvatska.hr

Cyprus
55 Avenue Eleftherion
Paphos 8021
Phone (357)99-858265

Czech Republic
Celostatni Kancelar Sluzeb A.A.
Ambrozova 729, 500 02 Hradec Kralove, Czech Republic
Phone zena: +420 773 138 303
Phone muz: +420 736 190 990
Website www.sweb.cz/aacesko

Denmark
Hovedservicekontoret
Att: Sekretariatet
Thorsgade 59, 3. tv.
2200 Kobenhavn N.
Danmark
Phone 45-3581 8531
Phone Helpline: (45)7010 1224
Website http://dkaa.dk

Europe (English Speaking)
Website www.alcoholics-anonymous.eu

Finland
Suomen A.A. Toimisto
Kielotie 34 C
Vantaa, 01301,
Finland
Phone (358) 9-8387040
Fax 503 2225-1430
Website www.aa.fi

France
Services Generaux A.A.
29 Rue Campo Formio
Paris, 75013
France
Phone 33-1-48064368
Fax 331-40210535
Website www.alcooliques-anonymes.fr

Germany
Anonyme Alkoholiker Gemeinsames Dienstburo
Waldweg 6
Gottfrieding Unterweilnbach,
D 84177, Germany
Phone 0049-(0) 8731-3 25 73-0
Fax 0049-(0) 8731-32 5 73-20
Website www.anonyme-alkoholiker.de

Great Britain
For Help with Drinking Problems
National Helpline: ***0800 9177 650***
Email Helpline: help@aamail.org

General Service Office
10 Toft Green
P.O. Box 1
York, YO1 7NJ
Phone 44-1-904-644026
Fax 44-1-904-629091

Northern Service Office **(Scotland)**
Baltic Chambers
50 Wellington St
Glasgow G2 6HJ
Phone 0141 226 2214
Fax 0141 221 9450

Southern Service Office
1 Raven Wharf
14 Lafone Street
London SE1 2LR
Phone (020) 7407 0700

Website www.alcoholics-anonymous.org.uk
Email AAInformation@gsogb.org.uk

Greece
4 Zinonos St. (Near Omonia Square)
Room 15 - 3rd Floor
Athens
Phone 210-5220416
Website www.aa-greece.gr

Hungary
General Service Office
Altalanos Szolgalati Irodas
PF. 258
Budapest 1536
Phone 36-1-2510051

Website www.anonimalkoholistak.hu

Iceland
National Service Office Of A A
P O Box 1149
Tjarnarata 20
Reykjavik 121
Phone (354)562-8812
Fax (354)562- 8814
Website www.aa.is

Ireland
Unit 2, Block C
Santry Business Park
Swords Road,
Dublin, 9,
DO9 H854
Ireland
Phone 00353 18420700
Fax 00353 18420703

Website www.alcoholicsanonymous.ie

Italy
Via di Torre Rossa 35
Scala B Int. 1B
Rome, 00165, Italy
Phone 39-06-6636629
Fax 39-6-6628334

Website www.alcolisti-anonimi.it

Latvia
Anonimo alkoholiku sadraudziba
Balta iela 7
Riga LV-1055
Phone (helpline) +371 27333523
Phone (GSO) +371 67333523
Website www.aa.org.lv

Lithuania
J.Basanaviciaus a.16
Birstonas, 59211, Lithuania
Phone (370) 319 45141
Website www.aalietuvoje.org

Malta
General Service Committee A.A. Malta
66 Archbishop StreetL
Valletta, , Malta
Phone 356 - 21-239264
Email help@aamalta.org.mt

Netherlands
Alegemeen Dienstenbureau A.A. Nederland
Statenweg 207
Rotterdam 3039 HP
Phone 31-10-243-0175
Website www.aa-nederland.nl

Norway
A.A. Servicekontor
Ullevalsveien 85 Bw
Oslo, 00454,
Norway
Phone 47-22-468965
Fax 47-22-468177

Poland
Biuro Sluzby Krajowej A.A.
Skrytka Pocztowa 243
00-950, Warszawa 1,
Poland
Phone 48 22 828 - 0494
Fax 48 22 828 - 0494
Website www.aa.org.pl

Portugal
Estrada Paco Do Lumiar, Bairro Horta Nova
Lote R4 - Loja A
Lisboa, 1600-543, Portugal
Phone (351) 21-7162969
Website www.aaportugal.org

Romania
Asociatia Biroul De Servicii Generale Ale Alcoolicilor
Anonimi Din Romania
Cluj-Napoca, str Dorobantilor 74, Bl. Y9, sc. 5, ap. 92. CP
400609
Romania
Phone (40) 774 021487
Fax (40) 374 490901
Website www.alcooliciianonimi.ro

Slovakia
Zdruzenie Pre Sluzby Anonymnym Alkomolikom
Misijny Dom
Kaluarska 3
Nitra, 949-01, Slovakia
Phone (412) 37-651-62
Website www.anonyme-alkoholiker.at

Slovenia
Anonimni Alkoholiki Slovenije
Linhartova cesta 13
1000 Ljubljana
Slovenia
Phone: (+386)1 433 82 25
Website: http://www.aa-slovenia.si

Spain

Avda Alemania 9-3 Izqda
Principado de Asturias
Aviles 33400,
Spain
Phone 34-98-5566345
Fax 34-98-5566543
Website www.alcoholicos-anonimos.org

Sweden

AA Servicekontor
Bolidenvagen 20
121 63 Johanneshov ,
Sweden
Phone 46-8-6422609
Fax 46-8-7148224
Website www.aa.se

Switzerland

Geneve 13, 01211, Switzerland
Phone 41-022-344-3322
Fax 41-022-344-3322
Alcooliques Anonymes
Suisse romande et italienne
Rte des Arsenaux 3C
CH-1700 Fribourg
Website: www.aasri.org

Ukraine
Ukraine A.A. Service Center
116 Heroyiv ATO Street
Poltava, 36023,
Ukraine
Phone: +38-096-527-87-52
        +38-099-928-93-78
        +38-093-573-03-55
Website: http://www.aa.org.ua

NORTH AMERICA

USA
Mail Address:-
P.O. Box 459,
New York, NY 10163
Phone 212-870-3400
Fax 212-870-3003

Location
11th Floor
475 Riverside Drive at West 120th St.
New York, NY 10115
Website www.aa.org

Barbados
Barbados Intergroup
P. O. Box 858E
Eagle Hall
St. Michael
Barbados
Phone 246 426-1600
Website https://aabarbados.org

Bermuda

Bermuda Intergroup Committees

P O Box WK 178

Warwick

Bermuda

Phone (441)297-0965

Website www.aa.bm

Costa Rica (unverified)

Oficina de Servicios Generales (Costa Rica)

Calles 7 y 9 Avenida 12

100 Metro Al Sur y 75 Al Oeste de Acueductos y Alc

San Jose, Costa Rica

Phone 506-222-5224

Fax 506-258-4715

English Speaking Costa Rica

Website: http://www.costaricaaa.com/

Cuba (unverified)

Oficina de Servicios Generales

Calle 27 # 156A E/C L Y M

Vedado

Habana 10400Â¢Ãª

Phone (53)7-8306172

Dominican Rep (unverified)

Oficina de Servicios Generales de A.A. (Dom. Rep.)

Calle 30 de Marzo No. 43

3er Piso

Santiago, Dominican Republic

Phone 809 241-2622

http://www.aacaribbean.org/drepublic.html

El Salvador

Website http://aaelsalvador.org

Guatemala/Antigua
Websitehttp://antiguaguatemalaaa.org

Mexico
Huatabampo No. 18
Colonia Roma Sur
Mexico DF, 06760, Mexico
Phone (55)5264 - 2406, (55)5264 - 2466, (55)5264 - 2588
Website www.alcoholicos-anonimos.org.mx

Nicaragua (unverified)
Oficina De Servicios Generales
Costado Sur Colegio Maria
Mazzarello Bo. Altagracia
Casa #8, Managua
Phone 505-2-662022
Fax 505-2-662022
Website https://nicaraguaaa.com

Other Caribbean
Useful website http://www.aacaribbean.org/

Panama (unverified)
Oficina de Servicios Generales (Panama)
Avenida Central-Espana Perejil
Edificio Rafael, 1er Piso, Oficina 103
Panama
Phone 507 225-3585
Fax 507 225-3585
Website http://www.aapanama.org/

Trinidad & Tobago (unverified)
General Service Office
L.P. #52 Rivulet Road
Brechin Castle
Couva
Phone (868) 679-0066
Fax (868) 679-0066
Useful website
http://www.aatrinidadmeetings.yolasite.com/ Useful
website http://www.aacaribbean.org/

SOUTH AMERICA

Argentina
Oficina De Servicios Generales
Av. Cordoba 966 - Piso 11 J
Cidad Autonoma de
Buenos Aires, 1054 S.A., Argentina
Phone 011 4325-1813
Fax 011 4325-0067
Website www.aa.org.ar
Email osg@aa.org.ar

Bolivia

Junta de Servicios Generales de Alcoholicos Anonim
Calle Alcides D'Orbigny
Nro 95, Ofc. Nro 8
Santa Cruz, , Bolivia
Phone 59170046275
Fax 59170046275
Email osgbolivia@yahoo.com

Brazil

Junta De Servicos Gerais De A.A.
Av. Senador Queiroz 101 2 Andar
Conj 205
Sao Paulo 01026-001, Brazil
Phone 55-11-32293611
Fax 55-11-32293611

Escritorio De Servicos Locaisitm
Rua Dr. Telio Barreto
80, Sala 101 Centro
Macae 27910-060
Phone (55)22-2772420
Website www.alcoolicosanonimos.org.br
Email aa@alcoolicosanonimos.org.br
Website www.aa.org.br
Email aamacae@aa.org.br

Chile
Oficina De Servicios Generalesl
Bellavista 0330
Providencia
Santiago, Chile
Phone 556-2-7771010
Fax 56-2-7779013
Website www.alcoholicosanonimoschile.cl
Email aasantiago@tie.cl

Colombia
Oficina De Servicios Generales
Calle 50 #46-36
Oficinas 310, Edinicio Furatena
Medellin, , Colombia
Phone 57-4-2517887
Fax 57-4-2316458
Website www.cnaa.org.co
Email corporacionaa@une.net.co

Ecuador
Oficina de Servicios Generales (Ecuador)
Lorenzo Garaicoa #821
y Victor Manual Rendon 2 Piso, Oficina 208
Guayaquil, , Ecuador
Phone 593 4-2309023
Website www.aae.org.ec
Email alcohola@gu.pro.ec

Paraquay
Oficina de Servicios Generales
Ciudad de Lambaré,
Paraguay
Phone 595-21-907805
Fax 595-21-907805
alcoholicosanonimosparaguay@yahoo.com

Peru
Asociación de Servicios Generales De A.A. del Perú
Jose Pardo De Zela 524
Oficina 301
Lima, 14, Peru
Phone (51)1-2651847
Email osgaalima@hotmail.com

Uruquay
Oficina De Servicios Generales
Calle Salto 1291
Montevideo 100
Uruguay
Phone (598) 4-104592
Fax (598) 4-104592
Website www.chasque.net/aauy
Email aauy@chasque.net

Venezuela
Oficina de Servicio Generales (Venezuela)
Avenida Universidad, Esq. Coliseo Corazon de Jesus
Building J. A. Floor 3 - Office 34
Caracas, 01010, Venezuela
Phone 58-212-543-2286
Fax 58-212-541-8894
Website www.aanonimos.org.ve
Email osg@aanonimos.org.ve

AFRICA

Egypt
A.A. Egypt Intergroup
P O Box 195Cooki
Maadi
Cairo 11431
Phone (20)10-7130050
Website www.aaegypt.org

Ghana
Adenta Intergroup Central Office
New Adenta
C/O P O Box AF 405
Adenta Accra

Kenya
Phone (254)2-726530137
Website www.aa-kenya.or.ke
Email aa_kenya@yahoo.com

Rwanda
Phone (250) 78 43 68 176
Website www.aarwanda.org
Email info@aarwanda.org

South Africa
General Service Office (South Africa)
Units 5 & 6 Alves Centre
Jubili Streeet, Raceview
Alberton, 01449, South Africa

Postal Address:-
P.O. Box 2770
Alberton, 01450, South Africa
Phone 27-011-869-9077
Fax 27-8811-8699077

Website http://www.aasouthafrica.org.za/
Email gso@aanonymous.org.za

Tanzania
Dar Es Salaan Intergroup
P O Box 1678s
Dar Es Salaan
Email aatanzania@gmail.com

Uganda
A.A. Kampala Intergroup
Plot 1140 Salongo Kabanda Road
Kirinya-Kito, Bweyogere Re-xbitm
Kampala
Phone (256)772-674013
Email alcoholicuganda@yahoo.com

Zimbabwe
C/O Zimcada
#2 Drummond Chaplin St
Milton Park
Harare
Phone (263)4-741770
Website www.aazim.org
Email alalison@comone.co.zw

ASIA

Cambodia
Phone (855)12-222179
Website www.aacambodia.org

China
Alcoholics Anonymous China General Service Office
No. 38 Bei Luo Gu Xiang
Dong Cheng District
Beijing, 100009, China
Phone 86139-11389075
Website www.aa-china.org
Email gso@aa-china.org

Hong Kong
Flat A3A, 26/F
Pearl City Manison
22-36 Paterson Street
Causeway Bay
Phone (852)64305052
Fax (852)25242297
Website www.aa-hk.org
Email help@aahongkongintergroup.org

India
Rm 1 & 2 Municipal Eng. Schooltm
Behind Byculla Fire Brigade
Meghraj Shethi Marg, Bycullaa
Mumbai 400 008
Phone 91-22-23075134
Fax 91-22-2301-1517

Website www.aagsoindia.org
Email gsoindia@vsnl.com

Indonesia
Phone (62)361-756652

Japan
Tsuchiya Building 4 Floor
4-17-10 Ikebukuro
Toshima-Ku, Tokyo 171-0014, Japan
Phone 81 3-35905377

Website www.aajapan.org
Email gsoj-int@ric.hi-ho.ne.jp

Korea
RM #503 CHUNIL BLDG
69-13 TAEPYUNGRO 2-KA, CHUNG-KU
SEOUL, 100-861, KOREA
Phone 82-2-774-3797
Fax 82-2-774-3796

Website www.aakorea.co.kr
Email office@aakorea.co.kr

Mongolia
Amar's Street
Cultural Center Building
Room #422A
Ulaanbaatar
Phone 976-11-310448
Fax 976-11-310448
Website www.aa.org.mn

Philippines
A.A. Intergroup Angeles City
13-13A Sarita St, Corner Marlim Ave
Diamond Sub Division
Angeles City 2009
Phone (63)45-8924258
Website www.alcoholics-anonymous-philippines.org

Russia
Tayninskaya Street
House 8, Premise #2
Room 5,6,7
Moscow, 129345, Russia
Phone 007-095-1854000
Fax 007-095-1854000

Website www.aarus.ru
Email aarus@online.ru

Thailand
P O Box 1551
Nana Post Office
Bangkok 10112
Phone (66)2-2318300
Website www.aathailand.org

Turkey
Ziya Gokalp Bulvari 11
SSK Ishani A Blok, Kat 12, No. 921
Ankara, , Turkey
Phone (90) 312-4341223
Fax (90) 312-4957292

Website www.adsizalkolikler.com
Email info@adsizalkolikler.com

United Arab Emirates
P O Box 74169
Dubai
Phone (971)4-4143042

Website www.aaarabia.org
Email aainuae@hotmail.com

AUSTRALIA &
NEW ZEALAND

Australia
National Office Of Alcoholics Anonymous
48 Firth Street
Arncliffe, NSW 02205, Australia
Phone 61-2-9599-8866
Fax 61-2-9959-8844

Central Service Office Greater Newcastel Dist
Jesmond, NSW 02299, Australia
Phone (61) 2-49641555

Website www.aa.org.au
Email national.office@aa.org.au

New Zealand
Suite 11, Level 3
Anvil House,
138-140 Wakefield Street
Wellington 06011
Phone (64)04-4724250
Fax (64)04-4724251
Website www.alcoholics-anonymous.org.nz
Email nzgso@xtra.co.nz

UK Directory of Support

WALES

Dan 24/7 is a free and confidential drugs helpline
providing a single point of contact
for anyone in Wales wanting further information or help
relating to drugs or alcohol.

Call free-phone: **0808 808 2234**
http://dan247.org.uk/

SCOTLAND

Know the Score (Drugs Helpline)
Freephone: 0800 587 587 9
https://knowthescore.info/

Alcohol Focus Scotland
166 Buchanan Street
Glasgow
G1 2LW
Tel: 0141 572 6700
https://www.alcohol-focus-scotland.org.uk/
Email: enquiries@alcohol-focus-   scotland.org.uk

NORTHERN IRELAND

Addiction NI
Addiction NI is a Trading Style of The Northern Ireland Community Addiction Service, a registered charity providing treatment and support for people who are dependent on alcohol or drugs.
http://addictionni.com/
Telephone: (028) 90664434

ENGLAND

Talk to Frank (Drug & Alcohol)
The FRANK service is free, and operated by fully trained advisers. It provides information and advice and where to get support in your area for alcohol and drugs for both adults and children.

Freephone: 0300 123 6600
www.talktofrank.com

NATIONAL SUPPORT AGENCIES UK

(https://www.mind.org.uk/information-support/guides-to-support-and-services/addiction-and-dependency)

Addaction	National charity providing a range of services to help transform the lives of people affected by drug and alcohol problems - details of local services are available on the website.
Adfam	Support for family and friends of people with drug and alcohol problems
Alcoholics anonymous Helpline: 0800 9177 650	Fellowship of men and women who share their experience, strength and hope with each other that they may solve their common problem and help others to recover from alcoholism.

The Alliance **Helpline:** **0845 122 8608**	User-led organisation that provides information and advocacy for people accessing treatment for drug and alcohol problems.
Gamblers anonymous	Support groups for people with gambling addictions.
Gamcare **Helpline:** **0808 8020 133**	Free helpline offering advice, information and support for people experiencing gambling problems.
National Association for **Children of Alcoholics** **Helpline:** **0800 358 3456**	Provides information, advice and support for everyone affected by a parent's drinking, including adults.

National Problem Gambling Clinic 0207 3817 722	Treats problem gamblers living in England and Wales aged 16 and over.
Narcotics Anonymous 0300 999 1212	User-led group of men and women who support each other to stop using drugs.
Release **Helpline:** **0845 4500 215**	National charity that gives free and confidential advice about drugs and the law.
Sex and Love Addicts Anonymous	Support groups for people with sex and love addictions.
Smokefree	NHS information and advice to help stop smoking.

Talk to Frank

0300 123 6600

For information on drugs and getting help.

Turning Point

National organisation that provides health and social care services for people with complex needs, including alcohol and drug misuse and mental health problems.

27240710R00059

Made in the USA
Lexington, KY
28 December 2018